KALEIDOSCOPE

THE LOST COLONY OF
ROANOKE

by
Edward F. Dolan

BENCHMARK BOOKS

MARSHALL CAVENDISH
NEW YORK

Benchmark Books
Marshall Cavendish Corporation
99 White Plains Road
Tarrytown, NY 10591
Website: www.marshallcavendish.com

Library of Congress Cataloging-in-Publication Data
Dolan, Edward F., (date)
The Lost Colony of Roanoke/by Edward F. Dolan.
   p.cm.–(Kaleidoscope)
Includes bibliographical references and index.
ISBN 0-7614-1301-4
1.Roanoke Colony Juvenile literature. 2.Roanoke Island (N.C.)History Juvenile literature. [1.Roanoke Colony.] I. Title. II
Kaleidoscope (Tarrytown, N.Y.)
F229.D65 2001   975.6175dc21   00-049799

Photo Research by Anne Burns Images

Cover Photo: Granger Collection

The photographs in this book are used by permission and through the courtesy
of: Northwind Picture Archives: 5, 6, 9, 13, 17, 18, 25, 30, 33, 41. Bridgeman Art
Library: 10. The Granger Collection: 14, 21, 27, 29, 34, 37. Corbis: 22, 43.
Art Resource: 38

Printed in Italy

6 5 4 3 2 1

CONTENTS

A MYSTERY UNFOLDS

The English ship the *Hopewell* dropped anchor near tiny Roanoke Island on August 19, 1590. Roanoke lay among a string of islands just off a stretch of the North American coast. One day, this coast would belong to the state of North Carolina.

This old woodcut shows the colonists arriving at Roanoke with John White in 1587. White then returned to Great Britain to collect supplies for them. But he was unable to sail west again for several years.

Two of the *Hopewell*'s boats dropped into the water. Sailors rowed toward the sandy beach. Riding in the lead boat was bearded John White. He was the governor of a small British colony on Roanoke. He had brought a band of settlers here in 1587 and had then returned to Great Britain to fetch needed supplies for them. He had been gone for *three* years. War between Britain and Spain had kept him away.

But now he was back. He stared at the beach with puzzled eyes. Strange. There was no one waiting to greet him. Why not?

He was about to stumble upon one of the great mysteries in American history.

When John White returned to Roanoke Island, he found no one on the lonely beach to greet him.

THE BEGINNING OF A DREAM

It was a mystery that had begun with the English soldier Sir Walter Raleigh. It dated back to 1584 and his dream of founding a colony in the Americas for his nation. Britain had done little in the New World since its discovery a century ago by Christopher Columbus. The small island country had tried just once to start a colony there—and failed.

Sir Walter Raleigh was a famous writer and soldier. He wanted to bring new honor and wealth to Great Britain by founding a colony in the New World.

But now Raleigh stepped forward. He obtained the permission of Queen Elizabeth for the venture. Then, with money awarded him by the British queen, he sent two ships across the Atlantic.

Their crews spent the summer searching among the islands along the coast of the future North Carolina. One day, they stopped at a small island, called Roanoke after the Indians who lived there. On returning home, the seamen told Raleigh that it would be a fine spot for their country's first New World settlement.

Queen Elizabeth, known to her subjects as the Virgin Queen, pictured here with members of her court. Because she gave Raleigh permission to establish an English colony in America, he named the surrounding lands in her honor – Virginia.

11

TROUBLES ON
SEA AND LAND

In 1585, Raleigh sent a second expedition westward. Sailing aboard seven ships were upwards of 500 soldiers and workmen, including 108 colonists. They were to start the Roanoke colony by building a small fort and surrounding it with houses.

Their ships left England in April on a journey that was to be dogged by bad luck. First, a storm roared in overhead as the vessels were sailing past Portugal and scattered them in all directions. They did not reunite again until they were off the American coast. Then a sudden squall sent the main supply ship crashing into the shore. Its cargo of food, tools, clothing, and arms spilled into the boiling surf and was lost.

Bad weather dogged Raleigh's ships as they sailed westward to the New World coast. One of the most feared accidents that a storm-tossed ship could suffer was the loss of a mast.

13

WEAPEMEOC

Long, narrow islands separated Roanoke from the open Atlantic Ocean. Raleigh's ships dropped anchor near the outer islands. Then small boats carried the colonists and their supplies through a break in the outer island to their new home.

15

When the remaining ships finally reached Roanoke, the Indians welcomed them. But trouble erupted while the British were building their houses and the small fort. The cause of the problem was the food supplies that had been lost in the storm. The island had enough food for the Roanokes, but not for the newcomers. The two groups began to fight over the meager supply. In one skirmish, a Roanoke chieftain was killed.

The colonists had to defend themselves against the local Indians when the two groups began to compete for the island's food supply.

17

18

Surrounded by hostile Indians, the British remained on Roanoke until the summer of 1586. By then, they wanted no more of the Americas. Homesick and hungry, they sailed back across the Atlantic.

In the summer of 1586, the weary colonists sailed back to England. This is what the London dockside looked like at the time of their arrival home.

19

SETTLED AT LAST

Raleigh was disappointed with the failure to establish the Roanoke colony. But he was a determined man. He refused to give up his dream. In 1587, he organized another expedition. He chose 117 people—91 men, 17 women, and 9 boys—all poor and eager to start a new life somewhere else. To serve as their leader, Raleigh chose John White. White had been a member of the 1585-1586 expedition.

The settlers sailed west in May and went ashore at Roanoke on July 22. White marched them inland through the trees to the clearing where their houses stood waiting. Then they set about bringing all their supplies ashore, cleaning the houses, and making various repairs.

Made by an American artist three centuries later, this wood engraving shows the colonists arriving at Roanoke in 1587. The houses in the background are shown as closer to the shore than was actually the case at Roanoke.

21

They stopped working for a few hours on August 18. It was time to celebrate. That day, tiny Virginia Dare became the first British child to be born in the New World. Her parents were Eleanor and Ananias Dare. Eleanor was John White's daughter.

The colonists gather for the baptism of tiny Virginia Dare—the first British child to be born in the New World. No one has ever known how long she lived.

23

White had little time to enjoy his new grandchild. When she was nine days old, he sailed to England to obtain more supplies for the colony. He planned to return in a few months. But, on reaching home, he found that he would not be allowed to leave again until further notice.

Why? Because Spain was threatening war and planning to invade England with a fleet of 130 warships. The British government ordered all the nation's vessels to remain at home. They would be needed to defend the country.

One of the greatest sea battles in history— the British meeting with the Spanish Armada in 1588—kept John White from returning to Roanoke when he went home to England to collect supplies for the colony.

The Spanish fleet, which was called the *Armada*, lumbered into view on July 29, 1588. Dashing out to meet it went over 150 British ships. In the battle that followed, the huge Spanish galleons could not get past the fast-moving Britishers. The invaders finally ran out of ammunition and swung for home. As they fled, a storm caught them and sent many of the Spanish boats to the bottom of the sea.

Though victorious, England continued to keep most of its ships at home for fear of another Spanish attack. As a result, John White had to wait until 1590 before he could leave for the west again. When he did go, he did not travel as the head of a supply ship. Nor did he carry any supplies for the Roanoke settlers. Rather, he was forced to sail as a passenger aboard a British warship, the *Hopewell*, which was to scout the western Atlantic for Spanish vessels.

This British engraving of the battle with the Spanish Armada dates back to 1739.

WHITE'S RETURN

The date was August 18 when the two boats from the *Hopewell* brought White ashore on Roanoke Island. It should have been a happy day for him. After three long years, he was about to see his grandchild again. By wonderful coincidence, Virginia Dare was three years old that very day.

One of the strangest drawings ever made of the Roanoke story, this engraving shows Sir Walter Raleigh founding the colony in the name of Queen Elizabeth. However, it is a well-known fact that Raleigh never set foot on Roanoke.

This woodcut from the late 1800s considers the possibility that the Roanoke colonists died at the hands of local Indians while fighting over the scant food supply. But the truth of the matter is that no one knows why the colonists abandoned their New World home.

But White was troubled as he stood on the beach. There was not a soul in sight. Excited settlers should have been flocking around him with welcoming shouts.

White remembered that there had been trouble between the Roanoke Indians and the British over the island's scant food supply. Had it finally exploded in fighting? Had all his people died in the fighting?

White quickly led the *Hopewell*'s sailors inland to the clearing where the settlement had been built. Along the way, he looked for signs that a battle had been fought there. But there were none. There were no abandoned and rusting firearms. No skeletons.

He must have been stunned on reaching the clearing. It seemed impossible! The village had disappeared! Gone were the boards that had made up the walls and floors of the houses. All the doors and windows and chimneys had vanished. Not even a nail was to be seen, though there were a few rusted tools lying around. The place was surrounded by a wall built of logs.

Contrary to the reports that all the houses at Roanoke vanished, this drawing shows one cabin standing and, just beyond it, the chimney of another.

 At last! A clue to the possible fate of the Roanoke colonists. Carved into a tree trunk was the one-word message— CROATOAN.

What had happened to the village? Had the Roanokes burned it to the ground? That didn't seem possible. There would be blackened ruins if there had been a fire. But the clearing was clean and neat.

Then White smiled with relief. The settlers must have hauled everything away to be used in a new place. They had not left in a terrified rush. They had not been under attack. Trouble with the Roanokes may have been brewing, but his people had taken the time to pack all that was needed to start afresh elsewhere. They must still be alive in some new place.

But where? Within a few hours, White came upon what seemed to be the answer—a tree with a one-word message carved into its trunk: CROATOAN.

Named for the Indians who lived there, Croatoan was an island forty miles to the south. Unlike many of the Roanoke Indians, the Croatoans had always been good friends. White felt certain that the carving was a message left for him. His people were telling him where they had gone.

The next day he would solve the puzzle of his vanished friends and loved ones. He would have the *Hopewell* carry him to Croatoan.

This map by John White shows the positions of Roanoke and Croatoan islands. The map is part of a larger chart of the North American coast. White drew the chart sometime around 1585.

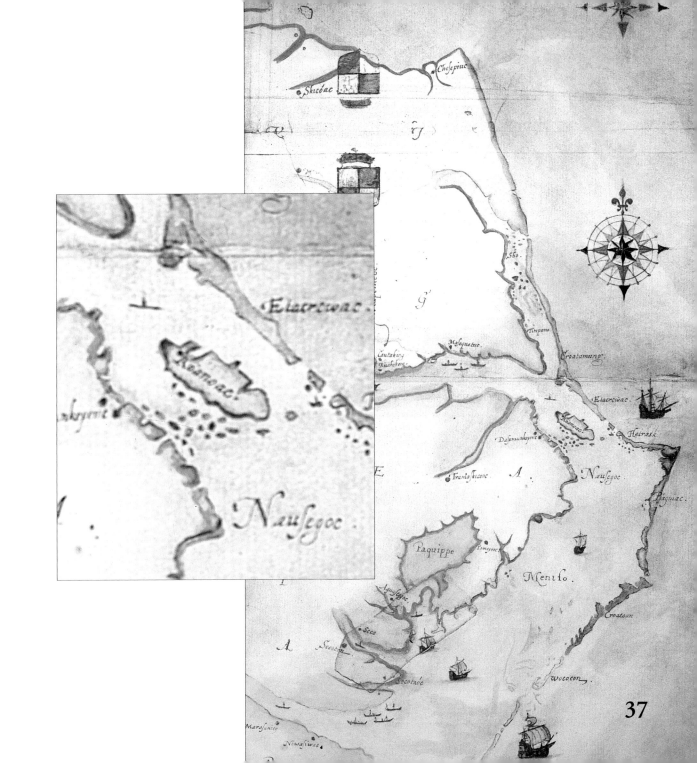

Skicóac

Chefepiuc

Elacrewac

Sho

Cautakuy
Rixahokene

Maſequetuc

Tripans

Croatamung

Elacrewac

Roanoac

Hatrask

Dafemunkepeuc

Tranſkecooe

Naueegoc

Paquiac

Paquippe

Tomcooroe

Meníſo

Aquoſcogoc

Croatoan

Seca

Secoton

Secotaóc

Wococon

Maraſuncen

Newaſiwac

37

38

A MYSTERY FOR THE CENTURIES

But White was cheated of the journey to the island. That night, just as the *Hopewell* was setting sail, a storm raged along the Carolina coast. The ship was blown out to sea and damaged.

A sudden storm—like the one shown here—kept John White from sailing to Croatoan. It blew his ship out to sea, damaging it so severely that it had to flee to the West Indies for repairs.

The next day, with the weather still bad, the captain refused to heed White's pleas to return to the coast. His ship was in desperate need of repairs. He set a course south to the West Indies, where they could be made. But heavy winds blew the ship off course. Battered and leaking, it finally made port in Britain.

The London dockside in the late 1500s when John White finally made his way home. White never learned the fate of his friends and family at Roanoke.

41

ON THIS SITE, IN JULY-AUGUST, 1585
(O.S.), COLONISTS, SENT OUT FROM ENGLAND
BY SIR WALTER RALEIGH, BUILT A FORT, CALL-
ED BY THEM:
"THE NEW FORT IN VIRGINIA"
THESE COLONISTS WERE THE FIRST SET-
TLERS OF THE ENGLISH RACE IN AMERICA.
THEY RETURNED TO ENGLAND IN JULY, 1586,
WITH SIR FRANCIS DRAKE.
NEAR THIS PLACE WAS BORN, ON THE 18TH
OF AUGUST, 1587,
VIRGINIA DARE,
THE FIRST CHILD OF ENGLISH PARENTS BORN
IN AMERICA—DAUGHTER OF ANANIAS DARE
AND ELEANOR WHITE, HIS WIFE, MEMBERS OF
ANOTHER BAND OF COLONISTS SENT OUT BY
SIR WALTER RALEIGH IN 1587.
ON SUNDAY, AUGUST 20, 1587, VIR-
GINIA DARE WAS BAPTIZED. MANTEO, THE
FRIENDLY CHIEF OF THE HATTERAS INDIANS,
HAD BEEN BAPTIZED ON THE SUNDAY PRE-
CEDING. THESE BAPTISMS ARE THE FIRST
KNOWN CELEBRATIONS OF A CHRISTIAN SAC-
RAMENT IN THE TERRITORY OF THE THIR-
TEEN ORIGINAL UNITED STATES"

1896

The captain promised that he would bring the saddened White back to Croatoan the next year. But White never returned to the New World. He tried to raise money for a voyage to Croatoan, with his every effort failing. He never solved the mystery of Roanoke.

Nor did Sir Walter Raleigh. He spent twelve years outfitting five expeditions and sending them west in search of the Roanoke settlers. Not one ship returned with news of the vanished settlers.

This monument, which was constructed in 1896, stands at Roanoke. It commemorates the founding of the colony and the birth and baptism of Virginia Dare. Also carved in the stone is the name of Manteo, the local Indian chief who befriended the colonists.

Over the years, however, historians have voiced several theories about the fate of the settlers. One theory holds that they moved north to Chesapeake Bay because they had heard of its good weather and were tired of the storms along the Carolina coast. They may have then settled among the Chespian Indians and, in time, taken up their ways.

If so, their lives would have ended tragically in the early 1600s. At that time, Powhatan, the leader of the Algonquian Indians in the region, went to war against the Chespians. He attacked and burned their villages. Not a single life was spared. Had the British been living among the Chespians, they, too, would have perished.

But no one knows whether these theories are true. All that can be said is that the fate of the first British people who tried to make their home in the New World remains a mystery.

TIMELINE

1584 Sir Walter Raleigh sends a scouting expedition of two ships to the New World. They land at Roanoke Island.

1585 Raleigh sends his second expedition to Roanoke to establish a colony there.

1586 The Roanoke colonists return to Britain.

1587 Raleigh sponsors a third expedition to Roanoke. John White serves as the expedition leader. Virginia Dare is born at Roanoke. John White sails home to England to obtain supplies for the colonists.

1588 War breaks out between Britain and Spain, preventing White's return west across the Atlantic.

1590 John White returns to Roanoke, finding the colony deserted. A storm forces him to leave for England before he can search further for the vanished people of Roanoke.

1590s–1600s Sir Walter Raleigh spends twelve years sending five expeditions in search of the lost colonists. Though the colonists are never found, some believe that they made their way north to safety when facing trouble with the Indians at Roanoke.

FIND OUT MORE

BOOKS ABOUT ROANOKE

Bosco, Peter I. *Roanoke: The Story of the Lost Colony.* Brookfield, CT: Millbrook Press, 1992.

Campbell, Elizabeth A. *The Carving on the Tree.* Boston: Little Brown, 1968.

Lacy, Dan. *The Lost Colony.* New York: Franklin Watts, 1972.

Tate, Suzanne. *Memories of Manteo & Roanoke Island, NC.* Nags Head, NC: Nags Head Art, 1988.

BOOKS ABOUT OTHER EARLY AMERICAN SETTLEMENTS

Dunnahoo, Terry J. *The Plymouth Plantation.* Parsippany, NJ: Silver Burdett Press, 1995.

Sakurai, Gail. *The Jamestown Colony.* Oakland, CA: LC Publishing Company, 1997.

Smith, Carter. *The Jamestown Colony.* Parsippany, NJ: Silver Burdett Press, 1995.

WEBSITES

The Colony of Roanoke
http://www.kidinfo.com/American_History/Colonization_Roanoke.html

Manteo & Roanoke Island History
http://www.outerbanks-nc.com/manteo/history/

The Lost Colony of Roanoke
http://www.ur.edu/~ed344/webquests/roanoke

AUTHOR'S BIO

Edward F. Dolan is the author of over one hundred nonfiction books for young people and adults. He has written on medicine and science, law, history, folklore, and current social issues. Mr. Dolan is a native Californian, born in the San Francisco region and raised in Southern California. In addition to writing books, he has been a newspaper reporter and a magazine editor. He currently lives in the northern part of the state.

INDEX

Page numbers for illustrations are in boldface.

Otros títulos de Finding My Way Books

Yo quiero ser como Joe Palomitas
Yo no sé si quiero un perrito
Marco y yo queremos jugar al béisbol
MyaGrace quiere hacer música

Kaitlyn quiere ver patos

Finding My Way Books

true stories of inclusion and
the development of skills
needed for self-determination

de Jo Meserve Mach y
Vera Lynne Stroup-Rentier

Fotografías de Mary Birdsell

Traducción de Karen Díaz-Anchante

Nuestra razón de compartir esta historia...

Kaitlyn tiene síndrome de Down. Kaitlyn tiene hermanas gemelas casi de su misma edad, por lo que es importante para todos en la familia tener la misma oportunidad de participar en las actividades que disfrutan. Los intereses de las tres niñas son respetados y atendidos. Los padres de Kaitlyn son capaces de apoyar las fortalezas y habilidades de Kaitlyn que mejoran su participación en actividades significativas, como ir al zoológico.

Nosotras elegimos escribir esta historia porque los padres de Kaitlyn muestran cómo fomentan habilidades que le ayudan a Kaitlyn a crecer para llevar una vida autodeterminada.

Nos sentimos honradas de compartir su historia.
~Jo, Vera and Mary

Una historia real que promueve
la inclusión y la autodeterminación

Finding My Way Books se dedica a celebrar el éxito
de la inclusión al compartir historias acerca de niños con necesidades
especiales en las familias y las comunidades.

www.findingmywaybooks.com

Es un día familiar en el zoológico.

Kaitlyn piensa que los mejores animales son los patos. A ella le encanta nadar.
A los patos también les encanta nadar.
Ella dice, "Vamos a ver patos".

Mamá piensa que hay muchos
animales divertidos.
Ella dice, "Vamos a ver a los monos".

Kaitlyn sólo quiere ver patos.
Ella dice, "Vamos a ver patos".

"Kaitlyn, ¿los monos están afuera o adentro?"
le pregunta papá.

Ellos están adentro.
Paige y Alexis encuentran al mono bebé.

A Kaitlyn le gusta ver caer el agua.
Es ruidosa y húmeda.
Esos monos son tontos.

Esos monos tontos no nadan.
"Vamos a ver patos", dice Kaitlyn.

Mamá ruge, "¿Quién vive al lado?"
"Los leones, los leones", rugen Paige y Alexis.

"Párense aquí cerca", dice papá.
"¿Pueden escuchar a los leones?"
No, los leones están durmiendo.

Esos leones soñolientos no nadan.
"Vamos a ver patos", dice Kaitlyn.

"¿Quién puede imitar a un elefante?",
pregunta mamá.

¿Tomarán un baño los elefantes?
No, hoy no.
Ellos juegan en la tierra.

Esos elefantes sucios no nadan.
"Vamos a ver patos", grita Kaitlyn.

"¿Quién quiere alimentar a las jirafas?"
pregunta mamá.

Alexis y Paige alimentan a las jirafas.

Esas jirafas hambrientas no nadan.
"Vamos a ver patos", ruega Kaitlyn.

"Ahora vienen las cabras y los osos", dice papá.
Kaitlyn mira a su familia.

A mamá le gusta hablarles a los animales.
A Alexis y a Paige les gusta alimentar
a los animales.

A papá le gusta ver todos los animales.
A Paige y a Alexis les gusta encontrar
animales bebé.

"Vamos a ver patos", dice Kaitlyn.

"Es el momento de ver patos", le susurra papá.

Oh, no, ¿dónde están los patos?

Papá ayuda a Kaitlyn a buscar a los patos.

Mamá ayuda a Kaitlyn a buscar a los patos.

Alexis y Paige buscan a los patos.
Ellas quieren encontrarlos para que los
vea Kaitlyn.

Kaitlyn busca también.
Kaitlyn ve algo gracioso.

Kaitlyn ve patos durmiendo.
Kaitlyn ve patos sucios.
Kaitlyn ve patos hambrientos.
Kaitlyn ve patos nadando.

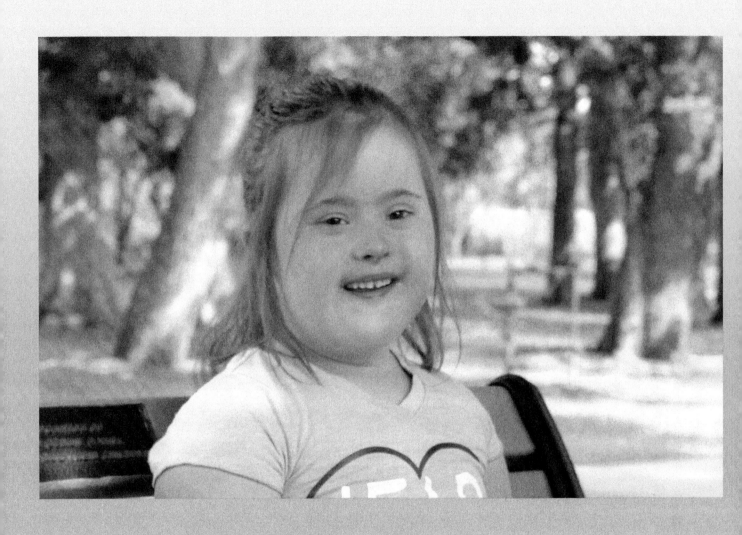

Kaitlyn está feliz.
Ella encontró a sus patos.

Gracias a Kaitlyn y a su familia por compartir su historia.

Índice de *Kaitlyn quiere ver patos*

Habilidades que promueven la autodeterminación que se ven en este libro:

Estimulando el desarrollo de la habilidad de autodeterminación en los niños

Nuestros libros están escritos en la voz real de un niño. El niño cuenta en su historia cómo está aprendiendo a ser más determinado por sí mismo.

A continuación algunos ejemplos de habilidades de autodeterminación:
· Libre elección
· Toma de decisiones
· Solución de problemas
· Establecimiento de metas y planificación
· Comportamientos de autonomía (autorregulación)
· Responsabilidad
· Independencia
· Conciencia y conocimiento de sí mismo
· Comunicación
· Participación
· Tener relaciones y conexiones sociales

Weir, K., Cooney, M., Walter, M., Moss, C., & Carter, E. W. (2011). Fostering self-determination among children with disabilities: Ideas from parents for parents. *Madison, WI: Natural Supports Project, Waisman Center, University of Wisconsin—Madison.*

Guía para la familia sobre cómo promover habilidades para la autodeterminación

Incentive la participación del niño y promueva los intereses de la familia:
Los niños son capaces de aprender más si participan activamente. Además, ellos desarrollan sus intereses a través de su participación.

Ir al zoológico es muy importante para los padres de Kaitlyn. Es una actividad que toda la familia disfruta. Sus padres han planeado cómo ayudar a Kaitlyn y a sus hermanas a disfrutar de las oportunidades que se les presentan en todo el zoológico. Su plan incluye las siguientes estrategias:

1. Ellos tienen una ruta planificada a través del zoológico de manera que los patos estén hacia el final de la ruta. Además, la ruta habitual asegura que las tres niñas encuentren animales que les gustan en cada visita al zoológico.

2. Ellos señalan animales y/o actividades en todo el zoológico. Ellos saben qué les interesará a cada una de las niñas. A Kaitlyn le gustan los patos. A Alexis le gustan los animales bebé. A Paige le gusta alimentar a los animales.

3. Ellos van al zoológico temprano por la mañana, ya que Kaitlyn está más contenta a esa hora, y hay menos gente en el zoológico.

4. Ellos van al zoológico con frecuencia por lo que es parte de la rutina habitual de las niñas.

Los padres de Kaitlyn saben que a ella le encanta el agua. Mientras la familia pasea por el zoológico, sus padres la incitan a buscar diferentes fuentes de agua, como por ejemplo, una cascada, charcos, fuentes de agua potable, mangueras rociando agua y fuentes de agua.

Lo que más le encanta a Kaitlyn son los patos, pero los otros animales que están en el agua también pueden captar su interés. Animales tales como hipopótamos, peces y caimanes facilitan una mayor participación de su parte a lo largo del tiempo que la familia pasa en el zoológico.

Actividades para el aula: *Kaitlyn quiere ver patos*

1. Describiendo animales:
Pídales a los estudiantes que identifiquen los cuatro animales descritos en el libro: monos tontos, leones soñolientos, elefantes sucios y cabras hambrientas. Haga que los estudiantes finjan que son cada uno de estos animales. Pídales a los estudiantes que compartan lo que saben acerca de otros animales que también podrían encontrar en un zoológico.

2. Descripción de la familia (Fortalezas e intereses):
Haga que cada estudiante haga un dibujo de su familia. Pídales a los estudiantes que le cuenten a la clase una cosa que a cada miembro de su familia le gusta hacer (interés) y una cosa en la que cada miembro de su familia es bueno (fortaleza). Pídales a los estudiantes que compartan lo que les gusta hacer juntos a los miembros de su familia.

3. Sentimientos:
Haga que los estudiantes cuenten a la clase sobre una vez en la que hayan tenido que esperar para hacer algo y cómo se sintieron al tener que esperar.

Jo Meserve Mach se desempeñó como terapeuta ocupacional por 36 años. Es una apasionada de la inclusión y el desarrollo de las habilidades necesarias para la autodeterminación y la independencia. Jo ve la inclusión desde una perspectiva funcional. Ella espera que estos libros compartan cómo los niños con necesidades especiales pueden estar activamente involucrados en su vida cotidiana. Incrementar la participación y la intervención de los niños y los jóvenes con discapacidades en las actividades familiares y comunitarias, enriquece la vida de todos. Ella cree que todos los niños tienen fortalezas increíbles que a veces sólo necesitan algunas adaptaciones ambientales para ayudarles a realizarse.

Vera Lynne Stroup-Rentier tiene 25 años de experiencia enseñando en las áreas de la Primera Infancia y la Educación Especial. Tiene un doctorado en Educación Especial de la Universidad de Kansas. Su trabajo actual como directora asistente del equipo estatal especializado en Primera Infancia, Educación Especial y Servicios de Profesionalización en el Departamento de Educación del Estado de Kansas le da la oportunidad de determinar y decidir sobre las políticas que afectan las vidas de los estudiantes con necesidades educativas especiales. Vera es una apasionada de la inclusión de todos los niños en lugares donde estarían si no tuvieran una discapacidad. Ella trae la perspectiva de la inclusión y la promoción de la autodeterminación de su trabajo con familias, profesores y terapeutas a lo largo de sus 25 años de carrera profesional. Criar a un adolescente y a un preadolescente con necesidades especiales enriquece su vida.

Mary Birdsell es una fotógrafa independiente y ex-profesora de expresión oral y teatro de escuela secundaria. Ella trae su talento en el arte y el diseño a nuestros libros. Mary se esfuerza por crear imágenes que reflejen las mejores cualidades de cada niño. Ella siente que una imagen puede proyectar la voz y las habilidades de un niño dentro de su ambiente. Su experiencia en la educación, el teatro y la fotografía se juntan al crear visualmente nuestros libros. Dentro de cada historia, ella utiliza colores y formas para promover el crecimiento del niño y el desarrollo de las habilidades necesarias para la autodeterminación, tal como se demuestra a través de cada historia.

Karen Díaz-Anchante tiene más de 20 años de experiencia enseñando lenguas – inglés en Perú, y español en los Estados Unidos. Tiene un doctorado en español en la especialidad de Literatura y Estudios Culturales Transatlánticos de Arizona State University. Actualmente es profesora universitaria de lengua, literatura y cultura hispanoamericana. Su interés por la traducción, la interpretación y la traductología la llevaron a involucrarse en el proyecto de traducir al castellano las historias infantiles que comparten los libros de Finding My Way Books. Como madre de dos niños pequeños, busca enriquecerse trabajando en proyectos con historias que promuevan el desarrollo de la autodeterminación, la personalidad y la independencia desde la primera infancia. Es también una ferviente creyente del efectivo poder de la lectura desde edad temprana.

41

Para más información
www.findingmywaybooks.com

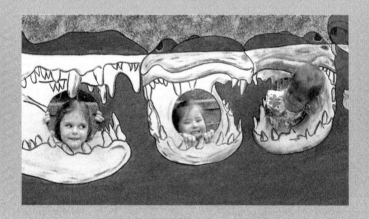

Póngase en contacto con nosotros
findingmywaybooks@gmail.com

CPSIA information can be obtained
at www.ICGtesting.com
Printed in the USA
LVOW05s1033191115

463308LV00009B/30/P